A Nifflenoo Called Nevermind

Margot Sunderland

Illustrated by

Nicky Armstrong

Routledge
Taylor & Francis Group

LONDON AND NEW YORK

O NE DAY, a Nifflenoo called Nevermind was walking in the park feeling very excited about going on his favourite swing.

But Ted the Tough was on it. "You can't have a go," said Ted with his tongue out, "because I'm not ever, ever coming off this swing."

"Never mind," said Nevermind, as he put his sad feelings about the swing inside his shorts.

Just then, up popped Nevermind's friend, called Colin Could-be-Worse. So off they went together to their favourite sticky bun shop on the corner.

But on the way, Nevermind fell into a puddle. "Could be worse," said Colin, "you might have broken your leg." "Never mind," said Nevermind as he put his yucky, wet feelings about the puddle into his pocket.

When they got to the sticky bun shop, they were just about to
tuck into some scrummy strawberry doughnuts when
Thumpa-Bot, who was standing close by, squished some jam
into Nevermind's hair.

"Never mind," said Nevermind, as he tried to swallow down his angry feelings about Thumpa-Bot with a big dollop of doughnut. But that meant that he got a very bad tummy ache indeed.

So to cheer themselves up Nevermind and Colin headed off
to the zoo.

When they got there it was closed.

"Could be worse," said Colin, "someone might have blown it up!"

"Never mind," said Nevermind, as he stuffed his fed-up feelings about the zoo into his sock.

And the next day, Nevermind's best friend went off him and got another best friend.

And the day after that, someone said that he smelled.

And the day after that, someone stole his water pistol.

And the day after that, he went swimming in the sea and trod on a jellyfish.

And each time, Nevermind said, "Never mind."

And each time, he found a place inside himself to put his feelings.

But after a while, Nevermind had so many cross and hurt and sad and worried and frightened feelings inside him, that he got stuck in a hedge.

"Could be worse," said Colin, "you might have got stuck in a prickly pear tree with a hungry bear underneath it." But for some reason, Nevermind didn't feel at all comforted by that.

Then along came a small red bogwert. The bogwert looked at Nevermind stuck there in the hedge and said, "If you want to get unstuck old chap, you've just gotta let go of some of your feelings."

Nevermind said that he couldn't possibly do that. "I've so many uncried tears inside me," he told the bogwert, "that it would cause huge floods. I've so much anger, that it would cause huge fires."

"It might seem that way," the bogwert replied, "but if you find a kind, safe person and tell them what you're feeling, it'll be just fine."

"And anyway, you can't go on like this. Look! Your feelings are leaking out of you." And sure enough, when Nevermind looked . . . they were!

When Nevermind looked, he saw that bits of his anger were leaking out in spiky little splats, making the daisies squeal and go "Ow!" and "Eek!"

And when he looked again, he saw that bits of his sadness had formed a sort of heavy grey fog, making some partying durds in the next field very unhappy, because bits the air had gone out of their balloons, and their birthday cake had gone all soggy.

The bogwert went on, "And what's more Nevermind, it's far too lonely and far too difficult to try to manage all of your feelings all by yourself. Let someone help!"

And because the bogwert was being so helpful, right there and then, Nevermind started to cry.

And there was a bit of a flood, but it was OK because it made some passing poppetywoos, who'd been looking for somewhere to have a wash, very happy.

And when Nevermind started to roar
with anger, some things did shake,
but nothing actually got
damaged or set on fire.

And at the end of telling the bogwert about all the feelings
he'd been carrying for *all* that time, *all* on his own,
Nevermind felt a lot, lot better and a lot, lot lighter.

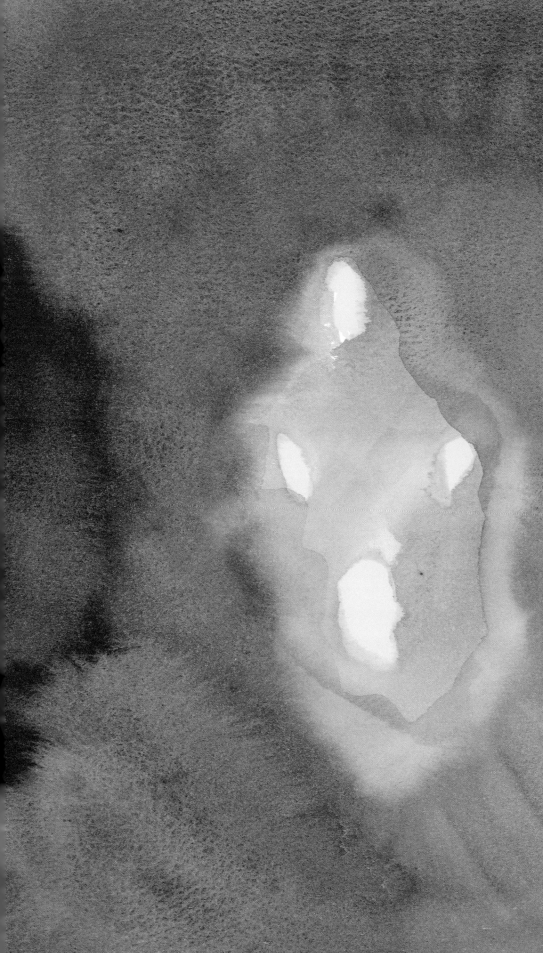

Then something amazing happened . . .

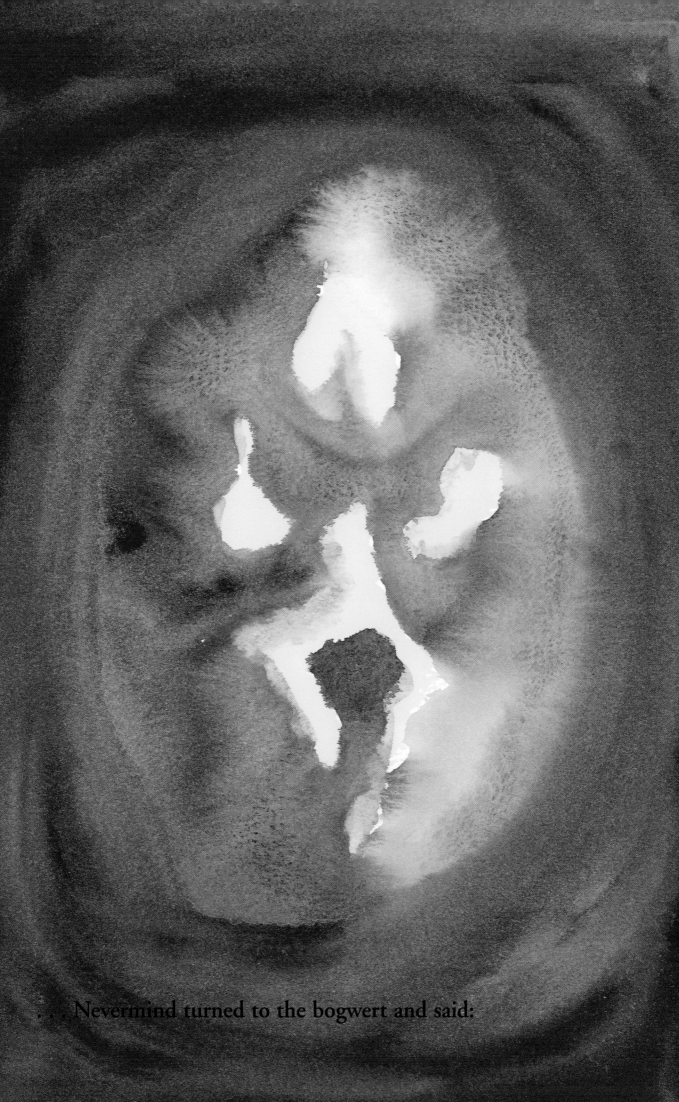

. . . Nevermind turned to the bogwert and said:

I

MI

And to this day, when Nevermind *minds*, he says so!

And Thumpa-Bot cleaned them so well that they sparkled and gleamed in the sun. And when no one was looking . . .

. . . Nevermind gave Thumpa-Bot a little nip on his nose.

And when Thumpa-Bot tried to squish jam into Nevermind's trainers, Nevermind said, "STOP!" so loudly that Thumpa-Bot actually said sorry, and Thumpa-Bot's mummy made Thumpa-Bot clean Nevermind's trainers.

And the bogwert taught Nevermind how to say to kind grown-ups, "I'm sad", "I'm hurting", "I'm scared". So the next time bad things happened, to do with swings, or puddles, or best friends, or water pistols, or jellyfish, or hedges, Nevermind remembered what the bogwert had said!

So the bogwert taught Nevermind how to let people know
that he minded, how to say very firmly to bullies, "No!",
"Stop!", "Enough!", and how it's best to ask for help from a
grown-up if someone far bigger than you is being horrible.

DO

NO!